IDEA STOLEN! UK TRADE MARK NEEDED

A HELP GUIDE WITH VIDEO INCLUDING SUBTITLES BY: A UK TRADE MARK NAME CREATIVE & COMPANY DIRECTOR

RENFORD MARSDEN

Wordsmith & Paper Limited

Legal Disclaimer

The publisher, author and our registered trade mark name in this book accepts no liability for this content therein relating to this topic of developing a UK trade mark name as a business owner of a UK Limited Company.

It is the readers responsibility to consider if they wish to follow this extensive help guide and work book.

Otherwise, seek out and engage an UK intellectual property attorney without delay to:

- accept their professional legal advice,
- understand their whole service process lead time from the beginning to end,
- get confirmation, approval that is included in Minutes of Meeting from the Board of Directors of the UK Limited Company,
- and give instructions in writing to proceed with your registration for a UK trade mark name,
- discuss staged payments to help your cash flow,
- agree and make payment of the professional fees.

Contents

Copyright	VII
Dedication	VIII
Foreword	XII
Mind Map - About this book	XIV
Introduction	XV
Mind Map: 1.0	1
1. A Lightbulb Moment	2
Mind Map: 2.0	10
2. Defining The Lightbulb Idea	12
Mind Map: 3.0	20
3. Got It, A Secret, The Cost	22
Mind Map: 4.0	25
4. Before You Start	26
Mind Map: 5.0	30

5. Dummy Run IPO Registration	32
Mind Map: 6.0	37
6. UK IPO Registration	38
Mind Map: 7.0	43
7. UK IPO Submission	44
Mind Map: 8.0	48
8. New UK Trade Mark Name	50
Mind Map: 9.0	53
9. The Madrid Protocol	54
Mind Map: 10.0	57
10. Marketing a UK Trade Mark Name	58
Acronyms	62
Bibliography	64
Resources	65
Conclusions	67
Endorsements	68
About Author	70
Image - Lightbulb	74

Worksheet: 1	75
Image - Ideas & Questions	76
Worksheet: 2	77
Image - Secrets & Value	78
Worksheet: 3	79
Image - Three	80
Worksheet: 4	81
Image - Are you ready?	82
Worksheet: 5	83
Image - Registration	84
Worksheet: 6	85
Image - Click	86
Worksheet: 7	87
Image - Trade Mark	88
Worksheet: 8	89
Image - Protocol	90
Worksheet: 9	91
Image - Marketing	92

Worksheet: 10

© 2022 | Wordsmith & Paper Limited | Renford Marsden | All Rights Reserved

It is not legal to reproduce, duplicate or transmit any part of this document in either digital, electronic means or printed format. Recording of this publication is strictly prohibited.

© 2022 | Wordsmith & Paper Limited | The Trainer Explainer | All Rights Reserved

It is not legal to reproduce, duplicate or transmit any part of the branded and watermarked explainer videos within this document in either digital, electronic means or printed format. Copying of these explainer videos is strictly prohibited.

Dedication

Key people have been major influencers in my 40+ years of a working life journey.

The most important of those is my wife Helen in supporting me on this project.

Equally, my brother Andrew and cousin and dear friend Mary Raftery.

Therefore, the following people who I have worked with have left a lasting impression of wisdom and support through the decades.

1970's:

- Mr. Stubbs - Bentalls.

- Ron Colton, Ted Tuck RIP – Decca Radar.

1980's:

- Sue Abbott - Page Aerospace

1990's:

- Claire Commins – Study Focus, Galway, Ireland
- John Curley – Entrepreneur & CEO of Curley Quality Food, Galway, Ireland
- Cyril Curley – Curley Quality Food, Galway, Ireland
- Keith Gardner RIP, Lizzie Potter - Brown & Root North Africa
- Dave Harrison RIP, Peter Jessup, Alan Ogunmuyiwa – Brown & Root
- Arthur van der Klaauw, Bert Landkroon, Evelyn McLean-Quick, Nick Webb - Halliburton
- Rt. Revd Bishop Sylvester Magro OFM RIP (former RC Bishop of Benghazi, Libya)
- Barbara Massey, Alan Massey – Occidental

2000's:

- Derek Glynn – Entrepreneur, Galway, Ireland

- Richard Card OBE, Sandy Gullis MBE, David Woolley, Andy Dawson, Mike Lyssy, Paul Fryer, Callum Morrison. - KBR

2010's:

- Derek Turner - GDF Suez UK

- Di Tate, James Evans, Jay Dhanecha, David Barber – Kent Police Service

- Chris Allington, Lyn Ballard, Phil Cramp – Eastergate Parish Council

2020's:

- Nathan Dring

For all the above I thank you for your amazing talent, energy and wisdom that has had a positive influence in those decades of my working life.

For those that have passed, you will never be forgotten and hence the reason you are mentioned as you work ethic and legacy lives on.

Special Mention:

To the amazing team of the **UK Intellectual Propert Office (IPO) at Newport, South Wales** who supported me during the challenging times of the COVID-19 restrictions in 2020.

Thank you for your patience and understanding when I telephoned with my technical questions relating to my UK trade mark name application.

Foreword

How Will This Book Helps You?

From the publisher, Wordsmith & Paper Limited perspective:

This business book written by a business owner who has taken a new brand idea and intellectual property in applying successfully for a UK trade mark name.

It is written for creatives or entrepreneurs that are business owners of UK Limited Companies.

Who may have been considering taking the business brand to the next level with thinking through an intellectual property idea in becoming a UK trade mark name.

This book has been designed for the reader to learn with the facts and references provided. Understand the whole process involved.

IDEA STOLEN! UK TRADE MARK NEEDED

Carefully designed mind maps with explainer video including subtitles – by using the camera on your smart phone to scan the QR code.

What is different about this business book is that it has the added value of worksheets for the reader to capture creative intellectual property to be considered and researched.

In addition, at the end of each chapter, you will have helpful information links to:

- Acronyms.

- Bibliography.

- Resources.

- Worksheet relating to each chapter topic, where the reader can brain storm ideas and understand the process to make the UK trade mark application process easier.

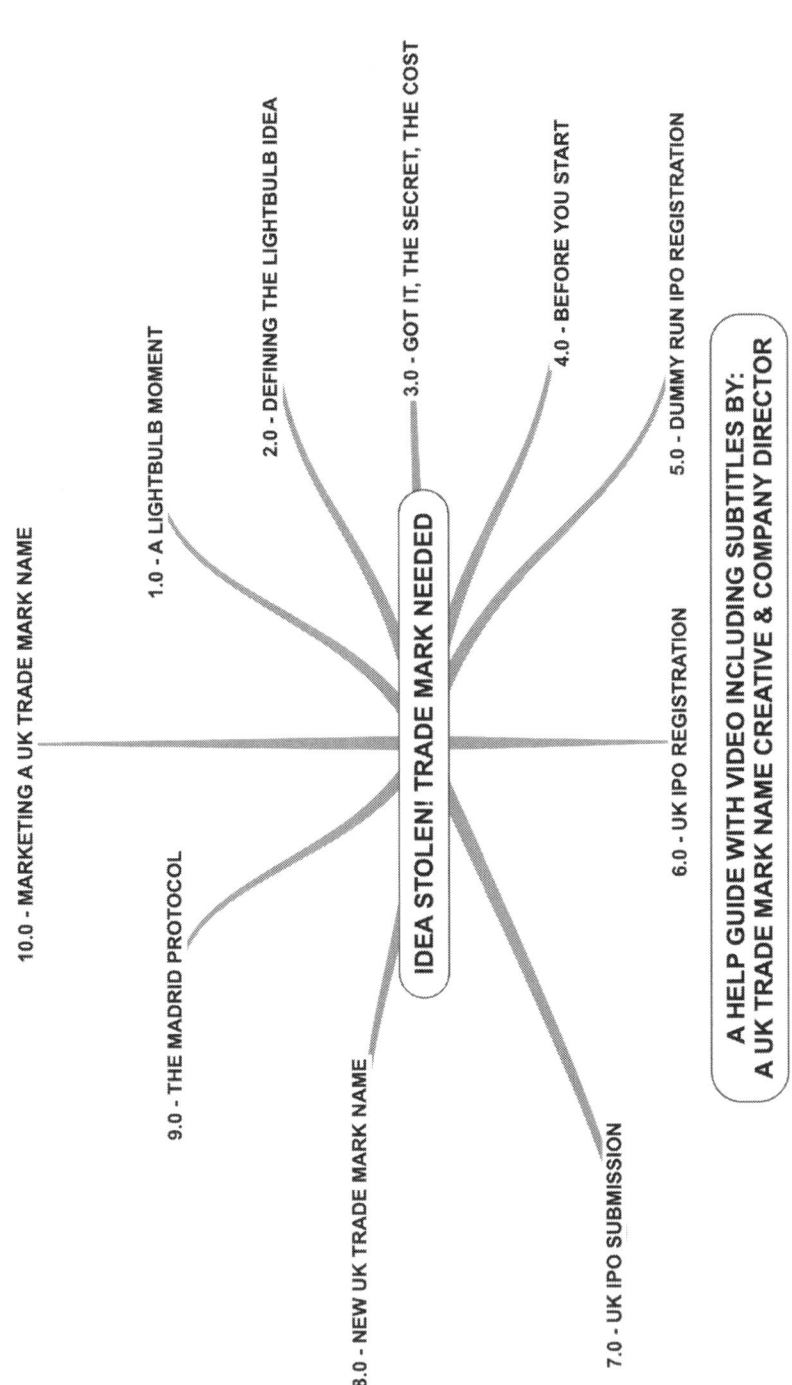

Introduction

Hello, my name is Renford Marsden and I am the writer or author of my first book.

This was a project with passion to be in the shoes of all creatives to cheish the dreams and ideas that need legal protection.

That as a Company Director of a small or medium sized business you can walk through all the processes and most importantly SAVE YOUR MONEY by D-I-Y.

Well, I was 60 years old in 2020 and a CEO of Wordsmith & Paper Limited that I founded in 2017 - I took the big leap of faith!

I deeply researched what the process was to make a successful UK trade mark name registration MYSELF without IP legal advice.

Understood what three words could work and what could not.

Then took a big leap of faith during COVID-19 UK lockdown of Spring 2020 to begin this amazing journey.

Thank you for seeking out this book and purchasing it from Amazon UK.

This topic is all about cherishing your Intellectual Property (IP) and from an idea taking it through the stages for it to become a UK trade mark name.

Sometimes, as a business owner and creative you could be:

- challenged,
- dismissed by people around you,
- that your idea means nothing,
- having self-doubt,
- that the whole process looks too complicated,

So, in what way will this content help you?

- I explain the process in small bite sizes

IDEA STOLEN! UK TRADE MARK NEEDED   xvii

- taking you through the Do's and Don'ts

- e.g., as it may look complicated, however it is a tried and tested solution.

This book will give you confidence in following your objectives or maybe pivoting your business with a new trade mark name.

It means something for you, because you have VISION and want to use the new trade mark name to:

- in gaining trust with a new brand brought to the marketplace.

Finally, your ideas and intellectual property is YOURS and therefore do not give it away. Please think carefully what you are sharing. As all has VALUE that benefiting someone else for gain or monetary value. All creatives with great ideas for commercial use can easily be disheartened and in the following pages will shine a light.

Reminder

Please. use the following pages for reference:

Acronyms

Bibliography

Resources

1. A LIGHTBULB MOMENT

- 1.1 - WHAT IS YOUR BUSINESS MODEL?
- 1.2 - WHAT DO CUSTOMERS WANT FROM YOUR BUSINESS?
- 1.3 - CAN YOU SOLVE THE CUSTOMERS PROBLEM?
- 1.4 - WHAT NEW SKILLS WILL BE REQUIRED FROM THE IDEA?
- 1.5 - IT HAS TO BE ORIGINAL & SIMPLE

Chapter One

A Lightbulb Moment

Key: 1.0 - Mind Map

1.0 - A LIGHTBULB MOMENT is that magic time of a new business idea that could be very beneficial. Where will it lead depends on what your business will need or want.

1.1 - Your existing business model will be already clear to you. However, with finding a new idea and how it will be integrated and expanded into your business is another matter. What are you trying to achieve and you must aim to cover the initial set-up costs involved.

1.2 - Top of mind is what your customers need and can your business provide the solution.

1.3 - Any customers seeking a product or a service is doing so to solve their problem. It is that simple! The new idea may or will offer better options which will bring more business.

1.4 - Any new idea may well need additional training to gain new skills and this has to be budgeted accordingly.

1.5 - All ideas have to be very simple, easy to understand and most importantly original. Therefore, not adapting or modifying another business idea. Otherwise, expect disappointment.

The main points to be considered to make this whole UK IP journey a success

A new UK trade mark name to brand your business can only work well as follows:

- keep it very simple,

- just three words can describe a UK trade mark name to brand your business,

- most importantly stay silent until the whole process is concluded successfully,

- must be thought through carefully and

how it will be applied to enhance your business objectives,

- thus, endorsing a concept to grow,
- future customers need to be able to understand the reasoning behind it,
- it will need to be added to your business plan for the UK Limited Company,
- depending on name and the profit it produces it will have value,
- your business bank may well be interested in supporting you once the IP application is a success,
- if you have a great idea then protect it and look to the future with excitement

Advantages of a UK Trade Mark Name

Top of mind that with this defined action will achieve the following:

- Protecting your business with a UK registered trade mark name is the key to brand success.

- It can ensure that you are the only business in your industry with that specific name.

- It can help to prevent others from using your registered name to sell their products.

- Once the name is registered, you will have exclusive legal rights to use these features in the UK.

- It can add intrinsic value to your UK incorporated company.

- Most important you are on safe ground to undertake legal action against anyone who infringes your rights in copyright.

The three main types of intellectual property:

- a patent protects a new way of making something,

- a design protects the look of something and

- a trade mark name protects the name of something - this is what is really important to define from the first instance

So how do you know which one you need?

- First get rid of any ideas that you think are already patented or registered,

- Any name not formally registered as a UK trade mark name can be copied and used without legal action,

Next choose the right level of protection for your business needs.

- if you are a one-man-band who is producing your product from your garage, a design patent might be the most suitable protection.

- If you are a business (UK Limited Company) with a reasonable to high turnover and a large volume of goods or digital services, then a registered trade mark name may be more suitable.

Time Limits on UK Patents and Trade Mark Name

Finally, remember that a patent can be applied for 10 years, but a UK trade mark name only lasts for the length of time you keep it - therefore use it immediately and market it wisely.

What is an incorporation?

- When you incorporate your business, you can protect your intellectual property within the protection of a limited company.

- Although you can apply for a patent and trade mark name by yourself, it is worth paying for the help if you do not have the time or confidence to undertake the registration process.

- A registered trade mark attorney will be able to draw up a detailed application, which means that you won't have to re-do the application yourself.

- If you decide to use a registered trade mark attorney, you will be asked to provide details of your business, including information on your products and the services you offer.

- Having a registered trade mark name, you can use it to protect your brand and prevent others from using your name to sell their own products.

- Your registered trade mark name, enables exclusive rights - which means that you are the only person who can use the mark on your products.

YOUR IDEAS ARE SO IMPORTANT - GO TO WORKSHEET: 1 - OR ON A SEPARATE PIECE OF PAPER:

Reminder

Please use the following pages for reference:

Acronyms

Bibliography

Resources

2. DEFINING THE LIGHTBULB IDEA

- 2.1 - WHAT THREE WORDS?
- 2.2 - WHAT MAKES THE THREE WORDS UNIQUE?
- 2.3 - SECRET RESEARCHING
- 2.4 - DEFINING THE IDEA
- 2.5 - DISCOVERED SOMETHING UNIQUE
- 2.6 - THINK ABOUT IT, DO NOT DELAY

Chapter Two

Defining The Lightbulb Idea

Key: 2.0 - Mind Map

2.0 - DEFINING THE LIGHTBULB IDEA.

The basic thinking with an INTELLECTUAL PROPERTY IDEA is using just THREE WORDS that attracts immediate business interest. What happens next is how you apply those words in a meaningful and rewarding deliverable from the creator to the end user or customer.

2.1 - It is critical to ascertain the WHAT THREE WORDS in a practical way by careful RESEARCHING and ANALYSIS. It is best practice to have a draft list of six different variables of those words.

2.2 - From the beginning aim to make the THREE WORDS so UNIQUE that it cannot fail in the submittal process to UK IPO.

IDEA STOLEN! UK TRADE MARK NEEDED

Spending loads of time writing it down and understanding what makes it STANDOUT from the business crowd.

2.3 - SECRET RESEARCHING is the most important lesson you will learn on this journey to having a successful discovery. It begins with setting PRIVATE MODE on your computer or using a safe SEARCH ENGINE: DUCKDUCKGO that does not use TRACKERS.

2.4 - Your THREE WORDS is a beginning of a concept to deliver something to add value to an end-user. You really have to map out the whole process that will make your business better and add value to your UK INCORPORATED LIMITED COMPANY. Be it large, small or a micro-business, the same values remains that understanding the AIMS and OBJECTIVES is critical to SUCCESS.

2.5 - Anything UNIQUE makes it special without a doubt. However, moving the IDEA and the THREE WORDS onward to establish that it HAS a FUNCTION and everlasting VIABILITY is what makes it SECURE.

2.6 - OVER THINKING can lead to PROCRASTINATION and SELF DOUBT. Think in the MINDSET of a CREATIVE and BELIEVE in your THREE WORDS. Please never RUSH a process like this and PLAN WELL. Avoid DELAYS and losing your UNIQUE THREE WORDS

The beginning of the UK IP journey

How to use a UK trade mark name to brand your business is as follows:

- been written in the shoes of this CEO, who created from concept a UK trade mark name: The Trainer Explainer®

- just three words can describe a UK trade mark name to brand your business.

- endorsing a concept to grow.

- if you have a great idea as a creative then protect it.

- we made a successful digital application and registration in 2020 to the UK IPO.

- our trade mark name is owned by Wordsmith & Paper Limited, incorporated in the UK in 2017.

When starting or pivoting to brand your business with a UK Trade Mark Name

When starting or pivoting a business, using a UK trade mark name can be

- the best way to protect your brand and
- ensure that you are easily identified by potential and current customers
- equally you are showing originality and a purpose to grow organically

What are your three words that could become your successful UK Trade Mark name?

Define what your business is:

- doing successfully currently is that sustainable,
- is there another possible business revenue stream that will work with a new trade mark name
- how can it work and be deployed successfully?

Discreet trade mark name key words searching methodology that leaves no breadcrumbs to be tracked

Have at least six sets of three words ready and here's your process steps:

1. set your internet browser to Private Mode (Apple Mac Desktop & Laptop Devices) or

2. correct your default internet browser to be DuckDuckGo (Why? - see Bibliography Section - please read first)

3. go to the UK IPO Trade Mark name search by key words (use your three words x 6 sets)

4. keep a record of your individual findings that includes date and time of each search

Researching, using significant words describing your service or product to the relevant class classifications

How your trademark words will be used within your business is defined by trade mark class classifications. These are made up of 45

IDEA STOLEN! UK TRADE MARK NEEDED

categories (Why? - see Bibliography Section - please read first)

Here are the process steps:

1. set your internet browser to Private Mode (Apple Mac Desktop & Laptop Devices) or

2. correct your default internet browser to be DuckDuckGo

3. go to the UK IPO trade mark classes searches (now use words that are mindful to what services/products will be achieved with the trade mark name)

4. find the relevant class or classes that are suitable to how your trade mark name will function and make a record of them.

YOUR IDEAS ARE SO IMPORTANT - GO TO WORKSHEET: 2 - OR ON A SEPARATE PIECE OF PAPER:

Reminder

Please use the following pages for reference:

18   RENFORD MARSDEN

Acronyms

Bibliography

Resources

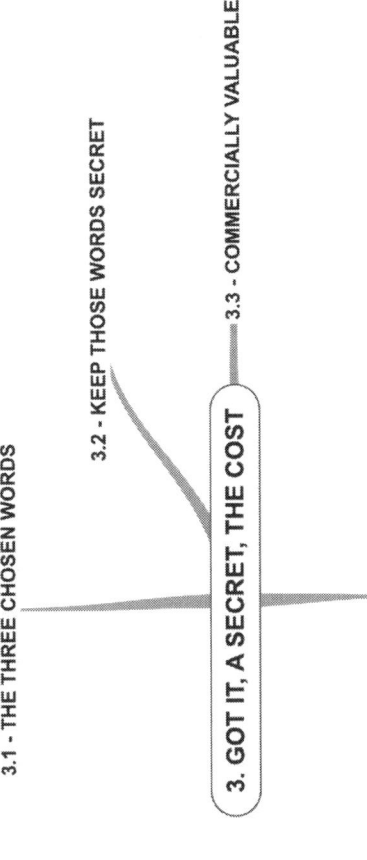

- 3.1 - THE THREE CHOSEN WORDS
- 3.2 - KEEP THOSE WORDS SECRET
- 3.3 - COMMERCIALLY VALUABLE
- 3. GOT IT, A SECRET, THE COST
- 3.4 - WHAT IS OUR BUDGET FOR UK IPO REGISTRATION?

Chapter Three

Got It, A Secret, The Cost

Key: 3.0 - Mind Map

3.0 - You have GOT IT in THE THREE WORDS and yet you must be very careful going forward.

3.1 - CONGRATULATIONS on your definitive THREE WORDS and no doubt you are very excited about the future. Please now treat this creation of an idea like a priceless piece of jewellery.

3.2 - THE THREE WORDS must be kept SECRET. Why? It is a very competitive marketplace for any UK TRADE MARK NAME. Thus, any other business getting advance notice because someone broke a PROMISE OF CONFIDENTIALITY and then let it slip can COST you dearly in COMMERCIAL TIME and MONEY LOST.

IDEA STOLEN! UK TRADE MARK NEEDED

3.3 - Any type of UK TRADE MARK are COMMERCIALLY VALUABLE. Therefore, DO NOT DISCUSS with THIRD PARTIES what you business is planning. An innocent conversation with someone you know could be repeated to someone you do not know or worse still a business COMPETITOR. Treat this like an item that you would lock up in the BANK SAFE that is protected against THEFT. COPYRIGHT THEFT is real and any CREATIVE or INVENTOR know the pain all too well.

3.4 - Set aside a realistic business BUDGET to cover all YOUR COSTS for the complete process. This should include a contingency fund for any objections after the UK IPO EXAMINATION process is concluded. Then THE THREE WORDS are published in the journal for public scrutiny and possible objections which is where costs come if you wish to defend.

Before you have finalised your UK trademark name idea, the key points to remember are:

- the IP words that you have found are clearly unique

- they must be commercially valuable with a positive business sales revenue outcome

- if your competitors were told these words, they would identify or recognise them without hesitation

- just remember you striving to improve your business and being a creative is an absolute gift.

YOUR IDEAS ARE SO IMPORTANT - GO TO WORKSHEET: 3 - OR ON A SEPARATE PIECE OF PAPER:

Reminder

Please use the following pages for reference:

Acronyms

Bibliography

Resources

4. BEFORE YOU START

4.1 - HAVE READY YOUR LIMITED COMPANY DETAILS INCLUDING COMMUNICATIONS ADDRESS FOR INSERTING INTO UK TRADE MARK IPO APPLICATION

4.2 - PLEASE READ THE UK IPO GUIDE (ONLINE OR PRINTABLE VERSION) ON REGISTERING A UK TRADE MARK

4.3 - CONSIDER CAREFULLY THE WISDOM OF PURCHASING A UK DOMAIN NAME BEFORE THE ACTUAL UK IPO REGISTRATION, AS IT MAY BE TOO LATE AFTER YOUR UK TRADE MARK APPLICATION IS PUBLISHED FOR PUBLIC SCRUTINY - SOMEONE ELSE COULD GET THERE FIRST!

4.4 - HAVE READY YOUR FINAL VERSION OF YOUR THREE WORDS FOR INSERTING IN UK IPO TRADE MARK APPLICATION TYPE (WORD) & TEXT (THE WORDS)

4.5 - HAVE READY YOUR FINAL VERSION OF YOUR CLASS TYPE FOR PRODUCTS OR SERVICES

4.6 - HAVE READY BUSINESS BANK PAYMENT DETAILS

Chapter Four

Before You Start

Key: 4.0 - Mind Map

4.0 - BEFORE YOU START is SAVING YOUR TIME and energy in making sure everything you need is readily available to make it easier

4.1 - LIMITED COMPANY DETAILS covering COMMUNICATION ADDRESS must match with UK COMPANIES HOUSE or UK HMRC address details.

4.2 - THE UK IPO GUIDE on registering a UK TRADE MARK is useful advanced reading to understand the whole process in detail.

4.3 - THINKING AHEAD, means does our business need a UK DOMAIN NAME? This will match our THREE WORDS of our new UK TRADE MARK. Honestly it is a RISK when you genuinely do not know if your UK IPO TRADE MARK NAME REGISTRATION will be successful or not. However, you will be kicking yourself if you are successful and a competitor has already purchased a UK DOMAIN NAME to block you from ever having a website to promote your idea.

4.4 - YOUR THREE WORDS is classified by the UK IPO as WORD TYPE and THE WORDS is TEXT.

4.5 - CLASS TYPES for PRODUCTS OR SERVICES. You have researched and identified what will make the UK TRADE MARK NAME work for your business.

4.6 - You now have an idea of the total cost to enable PAYMENT DETAILS. Have ready to hand for digital payment or other options.

This is an administration chapter and I appreciate most of us at director level know so much about governance and compliance.

However, if you are NEW BUSINESS OWNER to getting you different business addresses into the appropriate process steps described below.

Please bear in mind that you could have all or some of these business addresses:

- **communication address** - this type of

address is to ensure that letters arrive without delay and can be acted upon quickly. Such as:

- UK Government Agencies – UK Companies House, HMRC, UK Intellectual Property Office (IPO).

- UK Business Bank – to enable important letters to be issued acted upon in a timely manner.

- Company Accountant - will be issuing date and decision making critical information for a timely response.

- **registered office address** - this type is the formal address of the limited company and will appear on business stationary and websites.

- **delivery address** – as stated for products to be shipped to this location.

- **branch address** – customer focused contact points.

- **email address** – this would appear on your business website, business stationary and provided to UK Government Agencies to enable digital services and the added security thereto that is linked to it.

YOUR IDEAS ARE SO IMPORTANT - GO TO WORKSHEET: 4 - OR ON A SEPARATE PIECE OF PAPER:

Reminder

Please use the following pages for reference:

Acronyms

Bibliography

Resources

5. DUMMY RUN IPO REGISTRATION

5.1 - FOLLOW ALL THE STEPS IN 6.0 CAREFULLY ENSURE YOU SAVE AT EACH STAGE. DO NOT SUBMIT (YOU HAVE PLENTY OF TIME), AS YOU NEED TO BE COMPLETELY SURE OF YOUR NEEDS

5.2 - CLASSIFYING THE "NICE" WAY OF 45 CLASSES
- PRODUCTS - CLASSES 1 - 34
- SERVICES - CLASSES 35 TO 45

5.3 - ANY QUESTIONS?, THEN ASK THE UK IPO CLASSIFICATION TEAM

5.4 - HAVE YOU FUTURE PROOFED YOUR CLASSES?

5.5 - MORE CLASSES WILL LEAD TO MORE COSTS

Chapter Five

Dummy Run IPO Registration

Key: 5.0 - Mind Map

5.0 - DUMMY RUN IPO REGISTRATION is as stated going through the process on the UK IPO website and not committing to your submission.

5.1 - I have detailed the methodical process steps in mind map 6.0. Therefore suggest that you study this carefully.

5.2 - 45 CLASSES are split for PRODUCTS and SERVICES via NICE methodology and you need to research carefully.

5.3 - QUESTIONS on CLASSES, then you can make contact with the UK IPO CLASSIFICATION TEAM to seek guidance.

5.4 - CLASSES on not just for the PRESENT and you must consider FUTURE usage as well.

5.5 - COST OF CLASSES chosen may be in your budget or not. Be mindful of costs associated.

Now the journey begins to register your UK Trade Mark

A Trade Mark, design or business name can be registered with the UK IPO for a single fee.

First you must decide which level of protection you need:

- You can choose to apply for a Trade Mark, design or business name as a single application or you can apply for them all at once.

- If you choose to apply for them all in one go, you will need to pay an application fee of

- UK Trade Mark Forms and Fees detailed here (also shown on resources page)

- The application fee will be refunded if the application is refused.

If you want to keep your application confidential, you can choose to use the confidential filing option.

- You will also need to take a copy of the application to a Trade Mark office in person.

- Once the application is registered, you can apply for a Trade Mark, design or business name for free.

What type of UK business should I be looking at registering?

You should be looking into registering any business that you plan to use in the UK.

A UK Trade Mark Name registration does not automatically mean your business can use it.

How to Use It

- You can use a Trade Mark to protect your brand, but it will not prevent others using the same Trade Mark to sell similar products or services.

- The best way to prevent others from using a Trade Mark is to make it very difficult to copy your work.

- This can be done by making sure your

Trade Mark is distinctive or has high brand recognition.

Pivoting to protect your brand by using a UK Trade Mark

When starting or pivoting to brand your business with a UK Trade Mark Name

- the best way to protect your brand and
- ensure that you are easily identified by potential and current customers.

What is a UK Trade Mark?

- A Trade Mark type is a word, phrase, symbol or design that is used to identify a product or service and distinguish it from those of other businesses.
- It can be used on packaging, advertising and in business communications.
- Any Trade Mark type can be registered with the UK Intellectual Property Office (UK IPO) to gain exclusive rights to its use.

How to get a UK Trade Mark?

There are two ways to get a UK Trade Mark:

- apply for one yourself and register it with the UK Intellectual Property Office (UK IPO) to protect your logo, slogan and design.

- use a registered Trade Mark attorney - UK regulatory body of Patent Attorneys & Trade Mark Attorneys can help you seeking assistance

YOUR IDEAS ARE SO IMPORTANT - GO TO WORKSHEET: 5 - OR ON A SEPARATE PIECE OF PAPER:

Reminder

Please use the following pages for reference:

Acronyms

Bibliography

Resources

5. DUMMY RUN IPO REGISTRATION

5.1 - FOLLOW ALL THE STEPS IN 6.0 CAREFULLY ENSURE YOU SAVE AT EACH STAGE. DO NOT SUBMIT (YOU HAVE PLENTY OF TIME), AS YOU NEED TO BE COMPLETELY SURE OF YOUR NEEDS

5.2 - CLASSIFYING THE "NICE" WAY OF 45 CLASSES
- PRODUCTS - CLASSES 1 - 34
- SERVICES - CLASSES 35 TO 45

5.3 - ANY QUESTIONS?, THEN ASK THE UK IPO CLASSIFICATION TEAM

5.4 - HAVE YOU FUTURE PROOFED YOUR CLASSES?

5.5 - MORE CLASSES WILL LEAD TO MORE COSTS

Chapter Six

UK IPO Registration

Key: 6.0 - Mind Map

6.0 to 6.19 - In CHAPTER 5 MIND MAP it was suggested to carefully follow these 19 PROCESS STEPS and SAVE . This gives you time to check and make sure that this UK IPO REGISTRATION is perfect for your business. Not only in the NOW but for the FUTURE.

Here we go

How to register a Trade Mark, design, or business name

A Trade Mark, design or business name can be registered with the UK IPO for a single fee.

First you must decide which level of protection you need:

- You can choose to apply for a Trade Mark, design or business name as a

IDEA STOLEN! UK TRADE MARK NEEDED

single application or you can apply for them all at once.

- If you choose to apply for them all in one go, you will need to pay an application fee of
    - UK Trade Mark Forms and Fees detailed here
- The application fee will be refunded if the application is refused.

If you want to keep your application confidential, you can choose to use the confidential filing option.

- You will also need to take a copy of the application to a Trade Mark office in person.
- Once the application is registered, you can apply for a Trade Mark, design or business name for free.

Handy Hint: There is risk if you bulk apply (all at once) for more than one type of trademark as during the process. One of three could be challenged and thus have an impact on all. Think very carefully, about the impact to your business plan and the additional costs of waiting time.

What type of UK business should I be looking at registering?

You should be looking into registering any business that you plan to use in the UK.

A UK Trade Mark Name registration does not automatically mean your business can use it.

How to Use It

- You can use a Trade Mark to protect your brand, but it will not prevent others using the same Trade Mark to sell similar products or services.

- The best way to prevent others from using a Trade Mark is to make it very difficult to copy your work.

- This can be done by making sure your Trade Mark is distinctive or has high brand recognition.

When starting or pivoting to brand your business with a UK Trade Mark name

When starting or pivoting a business, using a UK Trade Mark can be

IDEA STOLEN! UK TRADE MARK NEEDED

- the best way to protect your brand and
- ensure that you are easily identified by potential and current customers.

What is a UK Trade Mark?

- A Trade Mark type is a word, phrase, symbol or design that is used to identify a product or service and distinguish it from those of other businesses.
- It can be used on packaging, advertising and in business communications.
- Any Trade Mark type can be registered with the UK Intellectual Property Office (UK IPO) to gain exclusive rights to its use.

How to get a UK Trade Mark?

There are two ways to get a UK Trade Mark:

- apply for one yourself and register it with the UK Intellectual Property Office (UK IPO) to protect your logo, slogan and design.
- use a registered Trade Mark attorney - UK regulatory body of Patent

Attorneys & Trade Mark Attorneys can help you seeking assistance

YOUR IDEAS ARE SO IMPORTANT - GO TO WORKSHEET: 6 - OR ON A SEPARATE PIECE OF PAPER:

Reminder

Please use the following pages for reference:

Acronyms

Bibliography

Resources

7. UK IPO SUBMISSION

7.1 - REGISTERED COMPLETED & UK IPO REFERENCE NUMBER ALLOCATED
REGISTER FOR EALERTS PROGRESS SERVICE PROVIDED BY THE UK IPO

7.2 - EXAMINATION OF APPLICATION BEGINS
AN EXAMINATION REPORT WILL BE SENT WITHIN THE LEAD TIME STATED ON THE UK IPO WEBSITE

7.3 - NOTIFICATION OF APPLICATION PRE-PUBLICATION

7.4 - PUBLICATION OF APPLICATION TO UK IPO TRADE MARK JOURNAL
PUBLIC CAN RAISE AN OBJECTION TO AN APPLICATION FOR A UK TRADE MARK - WHICH WILL INCUR LEGAL COSTS. 2 - 3 MONTHS IS ALLOWED FOR THIS PROCESS. PLEASE FOLLOW GUIDANCE FROM UK IPO WEBSITE

7.5 - NOTIFICATION OF REGISTRATION WITH UK IPO REFERENCE NUMBER & CERTIFICATE
EVEN AFTER SUCCESSFUL REGISTRATION THE UK TRADE MARK CAN STILL BE OPPOSED USING THE FOLLOWING CRITERIA: INVALIDATION, REVOCATION, RECTIFICATION, INTERVENTION. PLEASE FOLLOW GUIDANCE FROM UK IPO WEBSITE

Chapter Seven

UK IPO Submission

Key: 7.0 - Mind Map

7.0 - CONGRATULATIONS and now it is a waiting game.

7.1 - REGISTRATION SUBMITTED WITH REFERENCE NUMBER and strong advise that you insert your business email details to obtain alerts as to the ongoing progress through the stages shown in this mind map.

7.2 - EXAMINATION OF APPLICATION BEGINS which is due diligence of the content submitted.

7.3 - NOTIFICATION PRE-PUBLICATION which is advised to the original applicant.

7.4 - NOTIFICATION PUBLICATION OF APPLICATION which is advised to the applicant. The public now get an opportunity

IDEA STOLEN! UK TRADE MARK NEEDED 45

to understand the proposed UK TRADE MARK NAME and make observations or comments. Comments that have foundation may well delay your application and you must follow guidance from UK IPO website.

7.5 - REGISTRATION SUCCESSFUL and all the gateways have been passed through. However, be mindful that the new TRADE MARK NAME can still be opposed under certain criteria as described on the UK IPO website.

Your previous period of very heavy duty researching. Understanding very clearly where your idea will go. Knowing as a UK trade mark name has now reached an important stage. Equally, this is going to be an emotional journey as well and tempered with periods of frustration. However, learning the power of patience and thinking positively about the future will make this part easier.

Recognise that you have done a great job to clicking on the submission button and digitally sending your gem of an idea on its way.

What you do not know is that there are very gifted scrutineers with many years of experience that now will go through your application with a fine toothcomb.

Handy Hint: Be very mindful that this a due diligence process and have patience with understanding of a three months or more journey ahead.

Submission to Registration,

    1. Application Submission

    2. Application Examination

    3. Pre-Publication

    4. Application Published

    5. Registered

Handy Hint: It is critical that you take note and monitor each process stage understanding any actions to be undertaken by you as the applicant and responding in a timely manner.

YOUR IDEAS ARE SO IMPORTANT - GO TO WORKSHEET: 7 - OR ON A SEPARATE PIECE OF PAPER:

IDEA STOLEN! UK TRADE MARK NEEDED

Reminder

Please use the following pages for reference:

Acronyms

Bibliography

Resources

8. NEW UK TRADE MARK NAME

- 8.1 - WHAT IS YOUR SHORT TERM PLAN?
- 8.2 - WHAT IS YOUR LONG TERM PLAN?
- 8.3 - ARE NEW SKILLS REQUIRED?
- 8.4 - IS NEW TRAINING REQUIRED?
- 8.5 - SHOULD THE MADRID PROTOCOL BE CONSIDERED?
- 8.6 - UPDATE YOUR BUSINESS PLAN
- 8.7 - DO YOU NEED TO BUDGET FOR INITIAL ADDITIONAL COSTS?
- 8.8 - DO YOU NEED A SMALL LOAN FROM YOUR BUSINESS BANK?
- 8.9 - REMEMBER TO RENEW YOUR UK TRADE MARK AS ADVISED ON UK IPO WEBSITE

Chapter Eight

New UK Trade Mark Name

Key: 8.0 - Mind Map

8.0 - NEW UK TRADE MARK NAME WITH THREE WORDS and what is next on this journey.

8.1 - A SHORT TERM PLAN is so important to understand what will move this new UK TRADE MARK Name along. Set reasonable objectives.

8.2 - A LONG TERM PLAN is stabilising the foundations of the SHORT TERM PLAN. Again , ensure your objectives are realistic.

8.3 - You may have identified NEW SKILLS are required. These will be a new asset for enhancing this new trade mark name.

8.4 - You may have identified NEW TRAINING is required. They may be additional costs involved.

IDEA STOLEN! UK TRADE MARK NEEDED

8.5 - MIND MAP 9.0 is about THE MADRID PROTOCOL and carefully consider your options. Cost implications are involved and should be budgeted accordingly.

8.6 - A BUSINESS PLAN IS A MUST and will stand you in good stead with your business bank and possible future investors that support your new TRADE MARK NAME and BRAND

8.7 - ADDITIONAL COSTS BUDGET is very important if you are going to engage an UK IP ATTORNEY

8.8 - You may wish to discuss the need for a SMALL LOAN with your business bank. This will help with publicity, equipment and training costs.

8.9 - RENEWING YOUR UK TRADE MARK NAME is advised on set time period detailed on the UK IPO website.

UK Trade Mark Name Registration Complete

The final gateway stage has been completed and you receive confirmation email and a certificate attached to be proud of. You have made an idea to registered trade mark name happen. Be very proud of the journey undertaken with this successful achievement.

YOUR IDEAS ARE SO IMPORTANT - GO TO WORKSHEET: 8 - OR ON A SEPARATE PIECE OF PAPER:

Reminder

Please use the following pages for reference:

Acronyms

Bibliography

Resources

9. THE MADRID PROTOCOL

9.1 - FROM UK: WHICH COUNTRIES DO YOU WISH TO HAVE YOUR TRADE MARK?

9.2 - FROM UK: RESEARCH & SELECT A UK TRADE MARK (TM) ATTORNEY

EXCEPTIONS: NOT ALL COUNTRIES OUTSIDE OF UK CAN FILE UNDER INTERNATIONAL REGISTRATION. BUT MEMBERS JURISDICTIONS EQUATE TO MORE THAN 50% OF THE GLOBE - INCLUDING VIRTUALLY ALL MAJOR TERRITORIES

9.3 - CONFIRM THE LEAD-TIME FROM DATE OF FILING OF APPLICATION TO EXAMINATION IN EACH JURISDICTION (OFFICIAL TIMELINE IS 18 MONTHS FROM WIPO)

9.4 - AGREE THE PRICE WITH YOUR UK TM ATTORNEY

THESE FEES SHOULD ALSO INCLUDE OFFICIAL WIPO FEES (WHICH ARE PAYABLE BY YOUR TRADE MARK ATTORNEY IN SWISS FRANCS OR CURRENCY CODE = CHF)

9.5 - YOUR UK TM ATTORNEY WILL CONFIRM THE MADRID PROTOCOL SUBMISSION/REGISTRATION TO WIPO

9.6 - YOUR UK TM ATTORNEY WILL SUPPLY PROGRESS STATUS REPORTS

9.7 - YOUR UK TM ATTORNEY WILL ADVISE SUCCESS WITH WRITTEN CONFIRMATION RELATING TO SPECIFIC COUNTRY OR COUNTRIES (E.G. EU)

CERTAIN COUNTRIES, FOR EXAMPLE USA WILL ISSUE THEIR OWN SEPARATE CERTIFICATE

9.8 - YOUR UK TM ATTORNEY WILL CONFIRM REJECTION FROM SPECIFIC COUNTRY - DISCUSS POSSIBLE SOLUTIONS

ANY REJECTION MAY NEED TO BE PROCESSED BY YOUR UK TM ATTORNEY THROUGH THE SERVICES OF A LOCAL ASSOCIATE (TM ATTORNEY WITHIN THAT COUNTRY THAT ISSUED THE ORIGINAL REJECTION)

9.9 - HAVING ACHIEVED INTERNATIONAL REGISTRATION

IT IS POSSIBLE TO ADD OTHER COUNTRIES AT A LATER DATE. THUS, ALLOWING FOR EXPANSION. AGAIN, ASSISTING WITH THE SPREAD OF COSTS

Chapter Nine

The Madrid Protocol

Key: 9.0 - Mind Map

9.0 to 9.9 this mind map goes into so much detail on THE MADRID PROTOCOL. Please study and consider carefully the actions involved.

9.1 - WHICH COUNTRIES are you wishing to select for your UK TRADE MARK NAME to be successful and why.

9.2 - RESEARCH FOR A UK TRADEMARK ATTORNEY and choose

9.3 - APPLICATION FILING takes 18 months from WIPO

9.4 - PRICE, is understanding the fees involved with your UK Trade Mark Attorney.

9.5 - SUBMITTAL TO WIPO will be confirmed to you by your UK Trade Mark Attorney

IDEA STOLEN! UK TRADE MARK NEEDED

9.6 - STATUS REPORTS will be supplied by your UK Trade Mark Attorney.

9.7 - SUCCESS will be confirmed with appropriate documentation.

9.8 - REJECTION will be notified and your UK Trade Mark Attorney will advise a solution that may incur additional cost.

9.9 - AFTER INTERNATIONAL REGISTRATION it is possible to add other countries at a later date. Consider your options from a business perspective and discuss with your UK Trade Mark Attorney.

We professionally gave approved supplier status to Trade Mark Owners Association (TMOA) on post IP protection services.

- who provide amazing legal advice to protect our intellectual property of our UK trade mark name.

- were advised by TMOA about the Madrid Protocol System from WIPO and the timeline for this from the UK IPO approval date.

- thanks to TMOA amazing service delivery,

- based on our UK Trade Mark submitted via the Madrid Protocol System, we now have The Trainer Explainer Trade Marks in all of the EU countries.

YOUR IDEAS ARE SO IMPORTANT - GO TO WORKSHEET: 9 - OR ON A SEPARATE PIECE OF PAPER:

Reminder

Please use the following pages for reference:

Acronyms

Bibliography

Resources

10. MARKETING A UK TRADE MARK NAME

- **10.1** - WHAT WILL BE YOUR STRAP LINE WORDS?
- **10.2** - DO YOU NEED TO CONSIDER A UK TRADE MARK LOGO?
- **10.3** - WHO WILL BE YOUR IDEAL CLIENTS?
- **10.4** - WHAT EVENTS DOES YOUR IDEAL CLIENTS ATTEND?
- **10.5** - DO YO NEED A UK WEBSITE DOMAIN NAME?
- **10.6** - WHAT TYPE OF UK WEBSITE WILL BE NEEDED?
- **10.7** - WHAT ARE YOUR PRODUCTS OR SERVICES?
- **10.8** - WHAT ARE YOUR PRICES?
- **10.9** - WHAT ARE YOUR BRANDED COLOURS & FONTS?
- **10.10** - WHAT ARE YOUR SOCIAL MEDIA CHANNELS?
  - TWITTER
  - LINKEDIN
    - USER PROFILE
    - COMPANY PAGE
    - UK TRADE MARK SHOWCASE PAGE
  - FACEBOOK
  - INSTAGRAM
  - YOUTUBE
  - VIMEO
- **10.11** - HAVE YOU A SOCIAL MEDIA STRATEGY?
- **10.12** - HAVE YOU A MARKETING PLAN?

Chapter Ten

Marketing a UK Trade Mark Name

Key: 10.0 - Mind Map

10.0 - Marketing a UK TRADE MARK NAME includes may layers that need to be explained in this video with subtitles.

10.1 - Do you a need a STRAP LINE to qualify your new UK TRADE MARK NAME? Meaning: have you a few catchy words to explain the main objectives, for example: shop brands do this for advertising, making people curious to buy the product.

10.2 - A UK TRADE MARK LOGO could be considered to go with your UK TRADE MARK NAME. However, you have created your own design that is unique and simple. Then, undertake a separate UK IPO registration process and await a decision for many months.

IDEA STOLEN! UK TRADE MARK NEEDED

10.3 - With your UK TRADE MARK NAME can be turned into a recognised UK BRAND. Therefore, future clients will be attracted to this combination and what the UK TRADE MARK NAME is going to do for them. Basically, you NEED TO KNOW YOUR TARGET AUDIENCE and how you will SOLVE THEIR PROBLEMS.

10.4 - Meeting potential clients face to face is ideal if the atmosphere of the event creates no pressure, for example: Network Meetings, Trade Fairs or being a Guest Speaker. Conversations can begin and then see where it goes.

10.5 - YES, you need a UK DOMAIN NAME has to be chosen wisely. As it will be your digital shop window name for your website. Research well and be mindful of cost.

10.6 - Is the WEBSITE a digital window of INFORMATION with the latest BLOG and an ENQUIRY digital form for prospective clients to complete. Maybe, better still an ECOMMERCE WEBSITE for customers to simply CLICK and BUY PRODUCTS or DIGITAL SERVICES.

10.7 - Are your PRODUCTS or SERVICES range changeable and imaginative to ensure continuity? You have to consider what makes your range different from the competition.

This makes it a magnet for potential customers.

10.8 - Without stating the obvious your prices must be attractive. However, these price must be able to pay for your overheads and future proofing the business.

10.9 - Think carefully, in choosing colours and fonts that present well on various artwork. This MUST SHINE a POSITIVE LIGHT on your UK TRADE MARK NAME and create BRAND awareness.

10.10 - Genuinely, this is very subjective topic. You will gain lots of interest in you as a business owner and what your products or services are. Therefore, LinkedIn and Twitter must be first to consider because the business audience is huge. All the other social media channels is for various creatives and audiences. Please research wisely before dipping your toe into the water.

10.11 - Very useful to map out your SOCIAL MEDIA STRATEGY and then you have plan month by month. Also be in mind that some social media posts are evergreen and can be repeated without updating. This document will always be a revision document as you change the process.

IDEA STOLEN! UK TRADE MARK NEEDED

A MARKETING PLAN in 10.12 - is a discipline to ensure that you have objectives. Thus, helps with your PLANNED versus ACTUAL to understand what type marketing is working or not. This document will always be a revision document as you refine the process.

YOUR IDEAS ARE SO IMPORTANT - GO TO WORKSHEET: 10 - OR ON A SEPARATE PIECE OF PAPER:

Reminder

Please use the following pages for reference:

Acronyms

Bibliography

Resources

Acronyms

CEO: Chief Executive Officer

CITMA: The Chartered Institute of Trade Mark Attorneys

© : Copyright Symbol

D-I-Y: Do It Yourself

HMRC: Her Majesty's Revenue & Customs

ICT: Information Computer Technology

IP: Intellectual Property

IPO: Intellectual Property Office

NICE: International (NICE) Classification of Goods and Services as established by the NICE Agreement of 1957. This system is specified by WIPO.

MD: Managing Director

PTLLS: Preparing to Teach in the Lifelong Learning Sector

QR: Square Readable Image file that can be scanned to provide further information

® : Registered Trade Mark Symbol

SEP: Search Engine Providers e.g. Duck-Duck-Go, Edge, Firefox, Google, Safari

™ : Trade Marked Symbol

TMOA: Trade Mark Owners Association

UK IPO: United Kingdom Intellectual Property Office

USP: Unique Selling Proposition

WIPO: World Intellectual Property Organisation

Bibliography

Website Link (https://spreadprivacy.com/why-use-duckduckgo-instead-of-google/) to: Why Should I Use DuckDuckGo Instead of Google?

Source = DuckDuckGo

Website Link (https://www.marketingdonut.co.uk/marketing-strategy/branding/developing-your-usp-a-step-by-step-guide) to: Your USP - a Step-by-Step Guide

Source = www.marketingdonut.co.uk

Website Link (https://www.gov.uk/guidance/how-to-classify-trade-marks) to: How to classify UK Trade Marks?

Source = UK IPO

Resources

Website Link (https://www.youtube.com/playlist?list=PLPGicegzVCvENmAm2YhbQoxf_GNX9XHhk) to The Trainer Explainer Mind Maps on YouTube: THE TRAINER EXPLAINER| MIND MAPS: 1 – 10

Website Link (https://www.wipo.int/madrid/en/) to WIPO: Madrid Protocol System

Website Link (https://www.citma.org.uk) to CITMA: The Chartered Institute of Trade Mark Attorneys (CITMA)

Website Link (https://www.tmoa.com) to TMOA: Trade Mark Owners Association (TMOA)

Website Link (https://www.gov.uk/government/organisatio

ns/intellectual-property-office) to: UK IPO Office UK Intellectual Property Office

Website Link (https://trademarks.ipo.gov.uk/ipo-tmtext) to UK IPO – Key Word Search: UK Intellectual Property Office - Key Words Search

Website Link (https://www.gov.uk/guidance/search-uk-trade-mark-classes) to UK IPO – Trade Mark Classes Search: UK Intellectual Property Office - Trade Mark Classes Search

Website Link (https://www.gov.uk/government/publications/trade-mark-forms-and-fees) to UK IPO – Forms & Fees: UK Intellectual Property Office - Forms & Fees

Website Link (https://www.ipo.gov.uk/ip-support/welcome) to UK IPO – Training Resources: UK Intellectual Property Office - Training Resources

Website Link (https://ipreg.org.uk/) to UK Regulatory Body of IP Attorneys: UK Regulatory Body of Patent Attorneys & Trade Mark Attorneys

Conclusions

In conclusion, a UK trade mark name can only work well as follows:

- keep it simple
- must be thought through carefully and
- most importantly stay silent until the whole process is concluded successfully
- just three words can describe a UK trade mark name to brand your business.
- thus, endorsing a concept to grow.
- if you have a great idea then protect it and look to the future with excitement

Endorsements

I have known Renford Marsden

for some years now and have found him to be an intelligent person.

With great integrity and clarity, he is both pragmatic and careful with his guidance and thought process.

He has followed exactly the correct path for his own Intellectual Property rights.

The level of detail from

THE TRAINER EXPLAINER® explainer videos is clearly demonstrated.

This is evidenced by his excellent book, which will help in educating a wider audience.

Ken Sewell

IDEA STOLEN! UK TRADE MARK NEEDED

Head of Business Development

TMOA (1886) Limited

About Author

Founder

I am the CEO and founder in 2017 of a UK incorporated business Wordsmith & Paper Limited.

40+ Years Working Life

In my 40+ years of a working life I have been previledged to have the opportunities of working in different parts of the world.

Meeting amazing co-workers that shared wisdom and skills that I learnt from and then I was able to adapt and carry that batton further.

I have been lucky in various employments to help clients with delivering my taskings relating to change projects that made a difference.

My Lightbulb Moment

In 2020, The Trainer Explainer® - a UK registered trade mark name was born, enabling this idea to become a brand in it own right.

Life-Long Learning

With my PTLLS qualification I have enjoyed deliverying IT and software training to adults in different industries.

From an idea, then new skils that needed new learning and training has followed since 2020.

I believes in continuous personal development and increasing my skills set that will help future clients.

So over the years I have invested my time in going outside my comfort zone and it has opened more doors as a result.

Here is what can be achieved if the mindset is ready, willing and able.

Studying is so much harder later in life and at 59 years old I completed studying for a City & Guild qualification in Digital Marketing.

Social Media Channels

I can be found on:

- **Instagram** – you are more than welcome to follow.

- **LinkedIn** – you are more than welcome to submit a connection request with a message (please, quote this book page number) or just follow instead.

- **Twitter** – you are more than welcome to follow

I genuinely hope you have enjoyed this book and gained some insight.

Worksheet: 1

A Lightbulb Moment

PLEASE WATCH THE ATTACHED EXPLAINER VIDEO (BY SCANNING THE QR CODE). THEN, MAKE YOUR OWN NOTES ON THIS PAGE TO ASSIST DECISION MAKING

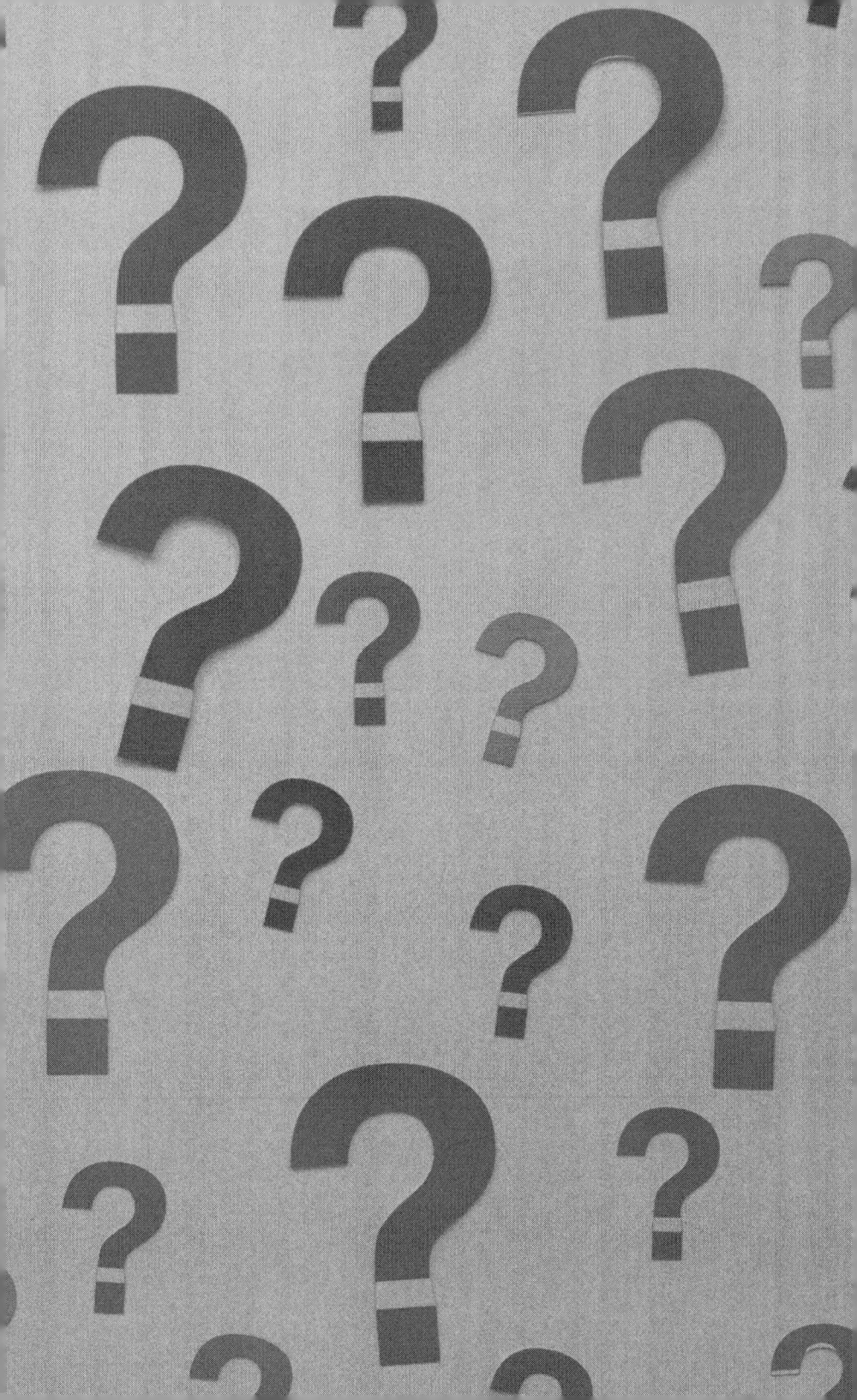

Worksheet: 2

Defining The Lightbulb Idea

PLEASE WATCH THE ATTACHED EXPLAINER VIDEO(BY SCANNING THE QR CODE). THEN, MAKE YOUR OWN NOTES ON THIS PAGE TO ASSIST DECISION MAKING

SECRET

£50

Worksheet: 3

Got It, A Secret, The Cost

PLEASE WATCH THE ATTACHED EXPLAINER VIDEO(BY SCANNING THE QR CODE). THEN, MAKE YOUR OWN NOTES ON THIS PAGE TO ASSIST DECISION MAKING

Worksheet: 4

Registering Your Three Words

PLEASE WATCH THE ATTACHED EXPLAINER VIDEO(BY SCANNING THE QR CODE) THEN, MAKE YOUR OWN NOTES ON THIS PAGE TO ASSIST DECISION MAKING

Are you ready

Worksheet: 5

Before You Start

PLEASE WATCH THE ATTACHED EXPLAINER VIDEO(BY SCANNING THE QR CODE) THEN, MAKE YOUR OWN NOTES ON THIS PAGE TO ASSIST DECISION MAKING

Registration

Worksheet: 6

UK IPO Registration

PLEASE WATCH THE ATTACHED EXPLAINER VIDEO(BY SCANNING THE QR CODE). THEN, MAKE YOUR OWN NOTES ON THIS PAGE TO ASSIST DECISION MAKING

Worksheet: 7

UK IPO Submission

PLEASE WATCH THE ATTACHED EXPLAINER VIDEO(BY SCANNING THE QR CODE). THEN, MAKE YOUR OWN NOTES ON THIS PAGE TO ASSIST DECISION MAKING

Worksheet: 8

New UK Trade Mark Name

PLEASE WATCH THE ATTACHED EXPLAINER VIDEO(BY SCANNING THE QR CODE). THEN, MAKE YOUR OWN NOTES ON THIS PAGE TO ASSIST DECISION MAKING

PROTOCOL

Worksheet: 9
The Madrid Protocol

PLEASE WATCH THE ATTACHED EXPLAINER VIDEO(BY SCANNING THE QR CODE). THEN, MAKE YOUR OWN NOTES ON THIS PAGE TO ASSIST DECISION MAKING

Worksheet: 10

Marketing a UK Trade Mark Name

PLEASE WATCH THE ATTACHED EXPLAINER VIDEO(BY SCANNING THE QR CODE. THEN, MAKE YOUR OWN NOTES ON THIS PAGE TO ASSIST DECISION MAKING

Printed in Great Britain
by Amazon